Brayton + Hughes Design Studio
The Art of Interior Architecture

Introduction by Jen Renzi

Edizioni Press

Brayton + Hughes

First published in the United States of America by
Edizioni Press, Inc.
469 West 21st Street New York, New York 10011
www.edizionipress.com

Printed in China

ISBN: 1-931536-18-X
Library of Congress Catalogue Card Number: 2002113984

Design: William van Roden
Editor: Sarah Palmer
Editorial Assistant: Aaron Seward
Cover Photo: John Sutton

Discoveries in Design
By Jen Renzi

Within the profession, architecture and interior design are often treated as two distinct and disconnected entities. Architecture, it's assumed, grapples with the serious stuff—matters of spatial organization, massing, structure—and plays straight man to its flightier cousin, whose purview encompasses the softer, decorative side of things—the drapes and tassels, if you will. Critical discourse about the subject furthermore perpetuates this perceived dichotomy, the myth that one medium picks up only where the other leaves off. Such narrow-minded thinking does a disservice to both disciplines—to say nothing of the end user, for whom it results in spaces that feel unresolved and disjointed.

The best designers make no such wholesale distinction between disciplines, but find fertile ground in the areas of overlap between them. They understand that creating the built environment is a hybrid art form: equal parts theater, sculpture, architecture, and—at its most inspired—poetry.

Brayton + Hughes Design Studio is such a firm. Co-founders Richard Brayton and Stanford Hughes see their craft as a meeting ground of architecture, interiors, and furnishings—of container and contained. In their view, the design process is an ongoing act of exploration and discovery, a repository for a diverse constellation of interests. It is an echo chamber across trades, a way of making connections between anything and everything that inspires them—from building materials, to schools of thought, to cultural traditions.

Brayton, Hughes, and their most recent partner, Jay Boothe, are trained as architects but prefer to work in the gray area where architecture and interior design bump up against each other. The firm's integrated, full-service approach acknowledges the porous boundary between two fields. Their methodology marries the best of both worlds, whetting interior design's free-associative way of thinking to a rigorous, linear architectural process. A simultaneous concern with minute details and the overall plan—and how the two fit together—leads to a highly nuanced and resolved body of work.

Brayton established the practice in 1989 after ten years with Charles Pfister at the Pfister Partnership. Hughes, a friend and collaborator since the two worked together at Bull Field Volkman Stockwell, joined the following year. "I was initially just going to rent Stanford a desk in my space," explains Brayton. "But it quickly became obvious that we knew all the same people and were competing for the same projects—while sitting in the same room. It fell into place that we should do this together." Jay Boothe, who serves as managing partner, joined the firm in 1996.

A network of contacts wasn't all the two had in common. Brayton and Hughes embraced a simpatico methodology and aesthetic sensibility. "We crawled out of the same tide pool of design," explains Hughes. "We're pretty interchangeable in terms of our skills, interests, and backgrounds." Their philosophy is largely informed by the traditions of Skidmore, Owings & Merrill. Pfister, Brayton's mentor, had worked in SOM's San Francisco office for 16 years prior to breaking out on his own. And Hughes directed SOM's interior design office during the 1980s. "We've patterned our business on that experience, especially in terms of a teamwork approach and pursuing diverse, high-end projects worldwide," says Brayton. As Brayton + Hughes expanded their office and the nature of their business began to change, Jay Boothe joined the firm. As managing partner, Boothe supports Brayton + Hughes' design philosophy, bringing his business and large-scale project experience to the company.

The designers and their 35-person staff also share a fascination with and commitment to exploring a full repertoire of stylistic vocabularies: traditional to contemporary, richly detailed to minimal-industrial. "It's important to not be a slave to modernism," says Brayton. "There's been great design in every period of history so that design has nothing to do with a particular period style," but the underlying ideas behind those stylistic traits. Brayton + Hughes' diverse body of work taps into a range of source material—from the Arts-and-Crafts traditions that informed the Disney Grand Californian Hotel in Anaheim, California, to the vernacular building type of Greek hillside villages, which influenced their design scheme for the Four Seasons Resort in Sharm El Sheikh, Egypt. Brayton + Hughes avoids a trademark style in favor of tapping into and communicating the essence of each client's philosophy, and answering the practical needs of the program.

Above all, the principals are united in their belief that the design process is an investigation, an opportunity to explore different cultures, artistic practices, materials, finishes, fabricators, and modes of expression. The intellectual act of investigation provides a conceptual framework for all their projects. "Our collective curiosity in design is what drives us—it's integral to the success of a project," says Brayton. "We are continually inquisitive about what different design opportunities—projects, clients, locales—have to offer." This enthusiasm leads to a remarkable diversity in the types of projects the firm chooses. Brayton + Hughes' client list spans all genres and multiple levels of scale: sprawling commercial complexes and pint-sized residential pied-à-terres; churches and embassies; international luxury resorts and local biotech laboratories. Even within a particular project type, clients may straddle extremes: financial clients, for instance, include Melchor Investments, a scrappy eight-person startup, and the well-established multinational McKinsey & Company, for which they have completed five commercial office projects.

"Our work is so eclectic," says Brayton. "It doesn't read as an oeuvre—it's more of an exploration than a stylistic body of work." This trademark eclecticism even accounts for the name of the business. "We called the firm 'Design Studio,' as opposed to Brayton, Hughes & Associates, to communicate that the practice is many people, working together on a number of different programs—some traditional, some experimental." The staff, divided equally between architects and interior designers, is amazingly nimble in its ability to juggle diverse projects, and even more diverse skill sets. "Everyone is dexterous, but has a certain strength," explains Hughes. Continually pursuing and executing a range of work leads to a vibrant cross-

fertilization of ideas. And avoiding tautology moreover keeps the partners fresh and interested in the business. "Doing work at different scales ensures that our design team doesn't get stale, or complacent, or pigeonholed."

While engendering Brayton + Hughes' eclectic output, the firm's sense of curiosity and exploration—as a design methodology—also accounts for its remarkable cohesiveness. There is a consistent tone from project to project, a level of craftsmanship, a purity of material expression, and a residential feel common to both traditional hospitality jobs, like the Hotel Del Coronado, and more contemporary interiors, such as the headquarters of Silver Lake Partners. This consistency owes to the firm's ideation process, structured around the search for an overarching metaphor to propel the program, from space planning to materials palette. "We come up with a central idea—sometimes a very simple one—and turn it into a lasting metaphor that will carry through the project," says Brayton. "It's a way to communicate our intentions to the client and come to an acceptance of a certain direction."

The exploration is a response to context, to idiosyncrasies of site and culture. "We search for what's unique about the project and the client, identifying a particular sensibility that's an asset," explains Hughes. Anything from corporate identity to the history of the base building becomes a source of inspiration. For the Four Seasons Resort in Egypt, the exploration entailed investigating ancient Bedouin textile traditions and meeting with an array of local artisans. Conceptualizing Schooner's Restaurant in Monterey, California, meant delving into the surrounding landscape's nautical heritage. "Sometimes the project just tells us what to do," says Brayton. "It's pretty obvious if a history and a story already exists. We can either follow it or juxtapose things against it."

And if the program doesn't inherently lead to a story or metaphor, they're not afraid to outright invent one. To execute the Ritz Carlton Half Moon Bay Resort, the design team wrote a mock-history, a fabricated narrative of the building, which is in the style of an early 20th-century Newport estate. Placing the concept within a historical framework, the designers discovered, helped the client envision the proposed direction. While treating their metier as a true art form, the principals never lose sight of the fact that their practice is, first and foremost, a business. Listening to the client and coming to an informed understanding of their specific needs and the way they process information is paramount to the firm's ongoing success.

Once client and project team agree on a guiding metaphor, the designers translate it into iconographic terms: a defining architectural gesture that crystallizes the overarching strategy. "Each project has a different inspirational spark, an inspired moment," explains Hughes. "We take an element and zoom it out to a larger scale." As an influence, Hughes cites Eero Saarinen's use of abstracted, form-giving metaphors—take, for instance, the swooping shape of the TWA Terminal, evocative of flight.

Brayton + Hughes likewise conjures dramatic, almost theatrical effects via stylistically succinct means: simple geometries, materials pushed to their formal extremes, an artfully calibrated wash of light. For McKinsey & Company's Palo Alto office, Brayton + Hughes referenced the client's Silicon Valley locale. Stylized tree sculptures that form the spine of a double-height staircase reference the history of the surrounding landscape, peppered with cherry orchards before the dot-coms took root. Wall cutouts along workstations allude to computer punch cards; textured glass panels throughout are etched with patterns recalling binary code—both nods to the Valley's reincarnation. For the offices and showroom of Boyd Lighting Company in downtown San Francisco, the building itself doubles as a light fixture: the massive, blocky façade is punctured with a staccato of glowing glass blocks.

Thanks to a concrete connection between the underlying ideas and their material execution, such moments never read as tacked-on ornamentation, but as an organic part of the whole. "It's artistic expression whetted to context in a very specific way," says Hughes. "We avoid mere appliqué."

Visually translating the metaphor into the overall design is not simply a matter of conjuring up isolated moments but of threading the concept throughout the interior. Done with a studied but subtle hand, these totemic details coalesce into an holistic composition, ensuring a carefully sequenced user experience. "The detail and the overall plan are equally important in our work," notes Hughes.

A unified spatial experience underlies all of Brayton + Hughes' projects. The firm is intensely preoccupied with how people use, move through, and interact within the confines of a given space. Most projects exhibit a strong sense of an almost civic scale: soaring double-height lobbies; well-thought-out circulation routes; common rooms that act as spatial organizers; multipurpose and adaptable zones; departments organized into infrastructural neighborhoods. Interstices are carefully resolved. "Circulation, even though it's the most anonymous of spaces, is also the most important in terms of spatial organization," says Brayton. "By taking into account the basic idea of scale, of events happening along a pathway, circulation organizes everything from cities to houses. It creates the basic idea of how rooms relate to one another."

To appreciate the full impact of their artistry, it is necessary to physically walk through a project. Much of Brayton + Hughes' attention is directed toward elements that are experiential and perceptual rather than merely visual. "The part of design we are most interested in doesn't have anything to do with how the project looks, but how it works," says Brayton. "Its function should support how the client's business works. Otherwise, we'd just be creating a glamorous shell."

To the designers, it's a moral imperative that the functional aspects of design—structure and infrastructure—can and should be an opportunity for a decorative statement. This sentiment is particularly evident in their approach to illumination. "The play of light is the single most important element in interior design," says Hughes. "Even the most beautiful interior won't live up to its potential if improperly lit." As such, every room of every project features three constituent parts: ambient, task, and the more atmospheric "sparkle" lighting. "Good lighting," says Hughes, "is both functional *and* perceptual."

About 60 percent of Brayton + Hughes business involves collaboration with other firms, including Ricardo Legorreta, Hill Glazer, Edward Larrabee Barnes, Moore Ruble Yudell, Hart Howerton, and Hornberger + Wurstel. Brayton + Hughes also enjoys a close working relationship with the in-house design staffs of hospitality giants Four Seasons, Ritz Carlton, and Hyatt. "One of the reasons architects like working with us is that we, too, are architects and approach projects architecturally," says Brayton. "We love the 'decorating' part, but it's always within the context of a strong architectural interior."

The success of such collaborative ventures, as well as independent projects, owes to Brayton + Hughes' embrace of interdisciplinary moments between architecture and interior design. Brayton cites Charles Pfister as a seminal influence in teaching him to look past the perceived limitations of the two mediums. "Architects and designers are trained very differently and, consequently, they don't always understand each other," says Brayton. "Decorators have a great way of perceiving things, and deal with aspects of design that architects never really understand or get to work on: acoustics, interior finishes, fabrics, pattern, texture, furniture, and lighting"—elements they delight in.

While Brayton and Hughes always strive to coordinate efforts when possible with fabricators, artists, and craftspeople, occasionally a project comes along that takes collaboration to another level. Disney proved a fascinating opportunity in this regard. "The client requested a Northern California, Arts-and-Crafts style building in the manner of Greene & Greene. But they also wanted to re-create the experience of creating it," says Brayton. The designers worked with hundreds of artisans and craftspeople on the project. "It was an interesting throwback to what it must have been like to work during the 1910s and 20s."

Brayton + Hughes' exhaustive connoisseurship and appreciation for a breadth of period styles has led to numerous historical commissions, among them San Francisco's Olympic Club, the landmark Hotel Del Coronado in San Diego, the Green Library Bing Wing at Stanford University, and St. Ignatius Church, for which the firm oversees an ongoing, multiphase renovation effort. Brayton + Hughes' strategy is to be sympathetic, rather than slavish, to history, while modernizing lighting and technology systems and overseeing seismic upgrades. Working in the office of Venturi, Scott Brown & Associates, from 1972 to 1979, Hughes had the opportunity to oversee two major restorations: the Pennsylvania Academy of Fine Arts and the Benjamin Franklin House. "The experience taught me a deep respect for historic architecture," and that historic integrity is less about nostalgically aping a period style and more about preserving a timeless, ahistorical essence of place. "We try to remove what was imposed on the building in an attempt to capture and renew its spirit," says Hughes.

There is a shared strategy between their historic projects and those executed in a contemporary vein. "There's a California-craftsman tradition, a use of materials and natural finishes, that always gets into our work—even the high-tech environments," says Brayton. "This use of wood and stone and natural materials creates a much softer kind of contemporariness."

Brayton + Hughes' complete integration of site and building, architectural envelope and decor, harkens back to earlier design traditions—the Arts-and-Crafts movement, the Bauhaus school, and the Wiener Werkstatte. Their artisanal approach and interdisciplinary philosophy recall a time when architecture was less hermetic, and existed in open-armed dialogue with other disciplines. Brayton mentions McKim, Mead & White as an aspirational ideal: "They integrated efforts very differently than we do today, working with other artists and artisans collaboratively," he marvels. "Art and design went part-and-parcel with great interior volumes and spaces." Such a mindset acknowledges that we experience space on a number of perceptual levels—visual, haptic, aural. By calling upon a range of artistic practices, and exploring a vast terrain of influences, the most inspired design taps into all the senses. Brayton + Hughes brings renewed relevance to this tradition.

DFS Group Limited—
Corporate Headquarters
San Francisco, California 1997

Brayton + Hughes designed 110,000 square feet of executive and administrative office space for the Duty Free Shops (DFS) Group, in collaboration with Fee Munson Ebert Architects. Store planning and product development departments were created on four floors of 525 Market Street in San Francisco. The top floor contains executive functions, including a boardroom, perimeter private offices, a training room, and legal and accounting libraries. Other floors accommodate a combination of private offices and open workstations, a large exhibition room for product display, product development rooms, fashion display and dressing rooms, and an employee lunchroom.

The overall design concept focuses on providing a backdrop for the DFS Group's specialty shop merchandise. A limestone feature stair and a circulation path at the building's core facilitate communication between departments and services. Coffee and copy stations serve individual departments at the corners of the main path on each floor. Beech veneer–clad columns with accent lighting line the main circulation path, providing a gallery of framed display surfaces for DFS Group merchandise and exhibiting photographs of their specialty stores.

Open workstations are organized to provide natural light and views of the city for the majority of employees. Ambient pendant up-lighting creates an optimal environment for computer work, while display accent halogen lighting in the merchandise design studios simulates the retail environment.

A The design of the reception area desk was inspired by a Japanese tonsu chest. Behind, a patterned, etched-glass screen separates the reception area from the rest of the offices.

As a nod to the DFS Group's large Asian market, a subtle Asian theme is expressed through silk wall panels and banquettes, in the tonsu chest–inspired reception desk, the credenzas, the video console, and in the artwork. Offices are framed by soffits, clerestories, and striped frosted glass sidelights. Materials include figured beech paneling, limestone and black granite flooring, frosted glass, integrally colored plaster, and fabric panels on walls and ceilings.

B

C

D

B **Banquettes in the reception lobby are backed with beech paneling, continuing the pattern in the reception desk.**
C+D **Open workstations allow natural light and city views to penetrate the office.** E **The boardroom features a curved, integrated console with a custom beech conference table.**
F **Circulation areas are bright and open, maintaining a feeling of lightness in the space.**

Reception Floor Plan

Boyd Lighting Company— Corporate Offices/Showroom
San Francisco, California *1997*

Boyd retained Brayton + Hughes to design its 11,000-square-foot head-quarters, which includes a showroom and office space. In their design, the architects manipulated space, daylight, and artificial light within an existing concrete shell to maximize interaction between certain departments, maximize privacy for others, and create a large open showroom that is dark enough to accommodate a variety of lighting schemes.

A canted wall plane filters light and bounds the showroom, while defining a separate full-height space that functions as an extension of the showroom, a gallery, a circulation element, and a gathering space for openings and other events. A translucent screen wall extends from the wall plane, acting as a giant light diffuser during the day and pulling light into the lower level spaces at night. This screen wall also illuminates the upper levels, which are separated in plan and section. Over the course of the day, the screen wall and the adjacent open space are animated by constantly changing light and shadow.

In order to reflect the company's transcendence of tradition, the architects took the opportunity to redesign the building's façade, while executing required lateral bracing. After filling four of the façade's large existing openings with concrete, they punched small openings and installed cast–blue glass in the spaces, to vary the color of light in the interior. The remaining larger openings manipulate daylight from the southern exposure and reinforce the central vertical plane.

A Holes filled with cast–blue glass were added into new shear walls to celebrate natural light on the inside.

A

B The building's entry doors are custom Corten steel. C The reception area. D The flexible "café" area can serve many functions and events. E The steel stair has a raw, industrial feel. F Typical work areas gain privacy from perforated steel panels. G A translucent wall carries light through the full height of the office, and is back-lit with skylights during the day. H The upper level balcony houses the café and private offices beyond.

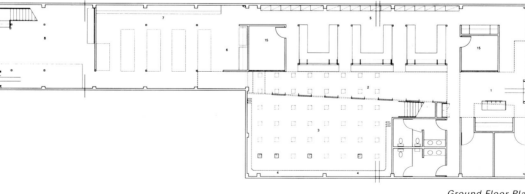

Ground Floor Plan

G   H

Pillsbury Madison Sutro—Law Offices
Palo Alto, California 1998

Brayton + Hughes designed 53,000 square feet on two floors of a build-to-suit facility in the Stanford Business Park. The program required perimeter offices for partners and associates, with open work areas for internal support staff and legal assistants. The program also required a centralized conference center flexible enough to support large gatherings and receptions, as well as scheduling and security, while additional program requirements included reception, a library, work rooms, a staff lunch room, centralized support facilities for mail distribution, a copy center, and additional satellite conference spaces, computer centers, and storage rooms. The client requested a design that responded to the need for increasing efficiency and flexibility in the firm's legal practice, as well as a space that would appeal to their high-tech Silicon Valley clientele.

To support the idea of efficient and flexible space, the design focuses on the concept of one-size-fits-all perimeter attorney offices, thereby departing from the traditional law firm layout that rewards seniority with larger offices. This was a major decision on the part of the client, and reflected the youthful demographics of the firm and the perception that their clientele shared similar notions of organizational behavior.

This approach resulted in an attorney-to-square-foot ratio of less than 500 square feet per lawyer. It also sponsored the firm's willingness to acquire new furniture for every office, providing built-in storage space and ergonomics. This created 30 percent more surface area and storage capacity than in the typical law office.

On a larger level, the firm was organized into team "neighborhoods," each with its own support and infrastructure, to foster teamwork and communication between all employees. Neighborhoods are grouped in the four quadrants of the building, with all corners reserved for open meeting space that is accessible to everyone.

Other innovations included downsizing the library and record storage in favor of increased information technology equipment, and outsourcing storage and printing functions. The main reception area stands as an exciting two-story symbol of the firm's success and hospitality, with a connecting stairway that fosters ease of communication between the two floors.

Materials included limestone, steel, glass, painted drywall, and wood paneling in select spaces, and state-of-the-art lighting and audio-visual systems.

A **The grand reception space gives a sophisticated and design-savvy first impression of the law firm.** B **The feature stair between the two floors fosters a sense of connection and communication within the office.**

A

C+D The feature stair is composed of solid wood treads and steel cable rails. E Translucent glass on the doors of offices maintains privacy while preserving the flow of light. F Wood paneling on open workspaces gives the space a warm feeling. G Circulation corridors are simple and elegant, expressing storage niches inside the private offices.

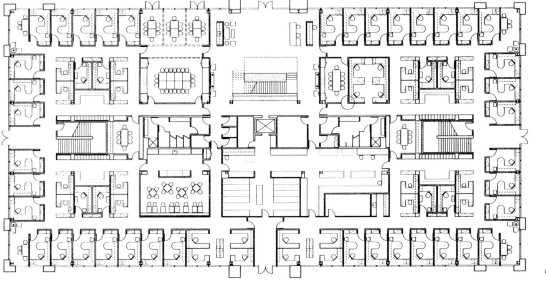

First Floor Plan

Chiron Corporation—
Life Sciences Building 4
Emeryville, California *1999*

Brayton + Hughes worked with Legorreta Arquitectos and Flad Architects on the design of this 280,000-square-foot research and development building for Chiron Corporation, sited in the industrial area of Emeryville. Providing programming, interior design, and furnishings for the public rooms, offices, conference facilities, and support spaces, Brayton + Hughes collaborated closely with the building architects to create a work environment that fostered a high degree of interaction and communication among scientists and staff. As this project was the first phase of a larger campus to come, the architects and designers strove to set the tone of collegiality from the beginning.

The resultant building organizes a series of atria, terraces, and public rooms into the workspaces, laboratories, office "cells," and conference rooms with monastic simplicity. A cloistered fellowship between the scientific researchers is expressed through the interior and exterior architecture. From a distance, the building appears as a monolith of cubist volumes, representing its interior functions through rich materials and painted surfaces. On the interior, interaction and communication are fostered through the incorporation of small office cells, which are only used for personal paperwork and teleconferencing. The design of the space encourages scientists to spend the majority of their time in the labs and public gathering spaces.

The private office cells are organized around a central interior courtyard on one side and are directly linked to the laboratories on the other. Opening onto the interior courtyard are public gathering spaces and break-out areas, which have been named "fellows rooms" in keeping with their intended use. Natural light enlivens and humanizes the interior spaces throughout.

Materials include warm earth tones of brick and plaster, stained concrete, and travertine. End-grain wood floors, accent walls in brilliant colors, and wood and leather furniture create an unusually humanistic work environment for a high-tech project of this nature.

A **The lobby features a collaboration of custom furniture designs by Brayton + Hughes and Legorreta Arquitectos.**

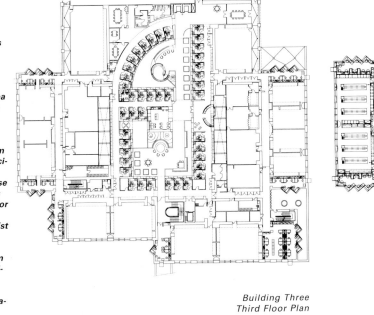

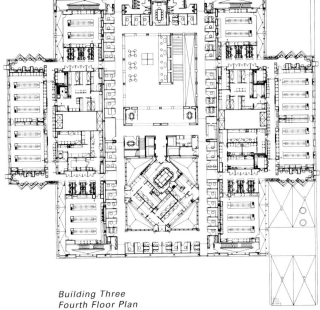

B **Lobby commons with scientists' offices beyond.**
C **The circulation hall through the administrative area features a view to the Berkeley hills in the distance.**
D **A break-out room in the atrium lobby.** *E* **Typical scientist's office.**
F **The multipurpose training room has views to an interior fountain.** *G* **The associated scientist team room with integrated furniture.** *H* **The atrium lobby is surrounded by scientists' offices, workrooms, and laboratories.**

Building Three
Third Floor Plan

Building Three
Fourth Floor Plan

G H

Global Consulting Firm
Los Angeles, California 2000

In their design of a new multi-floor office space for a global management consulting firm, the architects focused on creating a distinctive entry lobby, new conference spaces, and a work environment that would foster interactive relationships among employees. The program involved the expansion and renovation of 45,000 square feet of existing office space on several adjacent floors, as well as the modification of several communicating staircases.

Studies of the company revealed that the nature of its business kept many of its key personnel out of the office for extended periods of time. When in the office, employees tended to interact within mentorship groups rather than client teams, or to work individually documenting meeting notes and client strategies. To foster a new kind of interaction, the designers combined pods, containing living rooms, kitchens, and adaptable conference spaces, with individual work modules. The new plan also decentralizes support activities such as fax, copying, and supply storage.

Particular focus was placed on the entry lobby, which the firm hoped would express its global presence and gravity in the contemporary business market. A sleek aluminum wall and a global arc inscribed in the floor and ceiling lead visitors from the elevator lobby, along a horizontal timeline of materials celebrating the firm's 70-year history. The wall terminates at an interactive fiber-optic map of the firm's worldwide office locations, while the global arc suggests a relationship to a larger whole, symbolizing the firm's ability to draw from their worldwide pool of consultants. Arc and grid lines are defined in the floor, ceiling, and walls. The interactive map includes a web-based kiosk for accessing information about the firm, current stock quotes, and a featured history of Southern California business. Brayton + Hughes used this opportunity to create an interactive way to learn about the firm, focusing on the evolution and explosion of technology and business. A timeline of industry and business was created, covering the broad span of industrial and business ages, changing its faces, modes, and means—from ink wells to laser printers, from riveted iron plates to titanium fasteners, from cloth-wrapped cable to fiber-optic wire. The masses within the lobby space become a model of the multiple forces that are at work in a complex business organization, pushing and pulling one another in a dynamic growth process.

Materials for the entry and reception spaces are French limestone, terrazzo, Venetian plaster walls, beech, aluminum and other metal wall panels, acrylic, sandblasted glass, and polished aluminum.

A *The "global arc" inscribed in the ceiling of the reception area leads visitors from the elevators into and through the space.*

A

B *The entrance hall features a visual history of the firm.* C *Terminating in a fiber-optic map of the firm's world-wide office locations, the global arc serves as a technological compass to guide visitors.* D *The reception area is punctuated by a circular reception module.* E *Staff living rooms and kitchens combine with team meeting rooms for break-out and relaxation.*

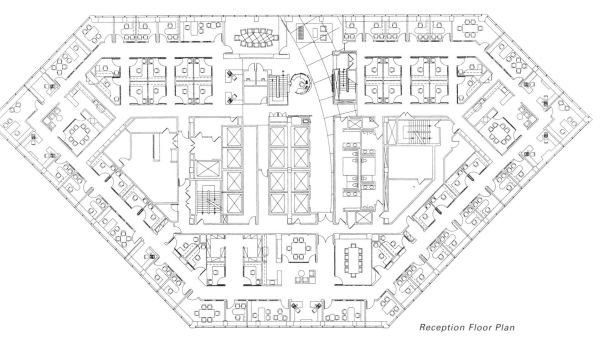

F Here, a typical associate's office is flanked by circulation with built-in filing storage. *G* The "team center" comprises a conference space, lounge, and kitchen. *H* The main conference room off the reception area features a custom conference table and cove-lit ceiling. *I* Detail of the team center.

Reception Floor Plan

Global Consulting Firm
Palo Alto, California *2000*

Brayton + Hughes created a plan for this 40,000-square-foot facility, which clusters work areas along gracious circulation paths defined by opposing visual elements. The office incorporates design motifs that reference the firm's participation in the regional transformation of Silicon Valley from pastoral orchards to the home of leaders in high-tech innovation.

One side of the corridor, a wall made of laminated glass panels, reflects binary code patterns in an arrangement of "1"s and "0"s that spells out the client's name. Opposite this wall, workstations are built against wooden "tree" elements that span the corridor and support the perforated metal ceiling.

The lobby stairwell is defined by an abstract sculpture of eight metaphorical trees, which becomes a natural trellis as the sculpture grows over the stair and into the skylight. Its eight-part trunk assembly is based on the eight-bit module of binary code. Referencing the unspoiled nature of the Valley's past and the advanced ideas of its present, the stairwell floor and walls are finished in rough quarried stone that is reminiscent of the sandstone rock formations in the area while remaining modern in style.

Materials used in the space are German fossil stone on the stairs, laminated patterned glass panels and perforated metal ceilings in the corridors, Venetian plaster on typical walls, beech on the workstations, sandblasted glass in the meeting rooms, bamboo flooring in the kitchen/lunchroom, and linear patterned carpet throughout.

A The reception lobby features a custom-designed desk and limestone floor. B Columns in the lobby are geometric, sculptural representations of trees, connecting the present, high-tech era of the Silicon Valley with its former, pastoral age of cherry orchards.

A

C

D

F

G

E

C *Custom support stations are integrated into ceiling supports and lighting.* D *Group work areas are organized into "pods."* E *The staff café and coffee center offers a place for breaks and socializing among employees.* F *Here, a group work pod is shown with its shared conference room.* G *The typical conference room has concealed high-tech teleconferencing equipment.* H *The two-story stair atrium is skylit from above.* I *The contemporary nature of Silicon Valley is reinforced by the system of eight—like the eight-bit module system of the binary code—that organizes the glass panels in the major circulation areas, and plays off the natural imagery of the stair sculpture.*

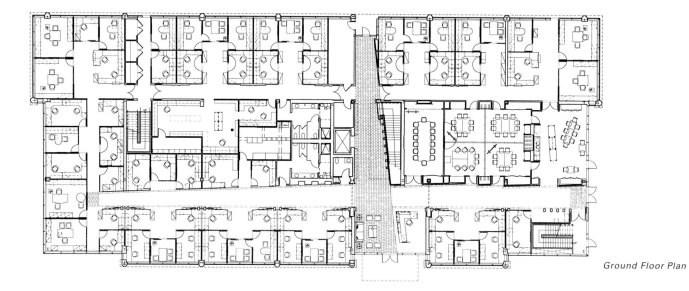

Ground Floor Plan

Forbes Silicon Valley Bureau
Burlingame, California *2001*

The Forbes Silicon Valley Bureau retained Brayton + Hughes when they leased 20,000 square feet of space in a new development adjacent to the San Francisco International Airport. The architects came up with a design that would consolidate Forbes' operations, previously scattered throughout the Bay Area. The program required private spaces for writers and editors, open studio spaces for graphic production designers, and team spaces for the advertising sales staff. Forbes also wanted an art gallery, which could function as a large party space, similar to the space in their New York office.

Rather than re-create the traditional interiors of Forbes' New York brownstone, the architects created a design that reflects the images and attitudes of Silicon Valley, providing a contemporary version of the Forbes yacht, Highlander, on the bay-front site.

Mirroring the curve of the base building façade in the bayside gallery, the design evokes the ship's shape. Simple, modern interior details provide a distinctly California aesthetic. Wooden beams and pilasters are veneered in basic hemlock, and painted wood plank ceilings echo the natural imagery. The floors are limestone and Palo Maria hardwood. Gallery display walls, upholstered in green fabric, are equipped with an anodized aluminum display rail for hanging artwork. A long steel display divider also provides surfaces for hanging artwork on both sides. It is clad in perforated panels that allow natural light to enter the gallery. The divider moves on recessed floor tracks, allowing the room to open up for banquets.

In contrast to the gallery's upscale finishes, the office areas are basic and functional. The design maximizes the amount of natural light in interior office spaces, which are furnished with open plan workstations for maximum future flexibility.

A The perforated steel space-divider can be hung with artwork on either side. Its perforations let light circulate through the space.

A

B The central
circulation hall is
designed as a
gallery featuring
artifacts from
Malcolm Forbes'
adventurous life.

B

C The entry features one of Malcolm Forbes' rare motorcycles.
D The steel display and divider moves along recessed tracks in the floor, allowing the entire space to open up for events.
E Office spaces are basic and simple.
F Art in the gallery is hung in front of a green cloth backdrop.

Floor Plan

Global Consulting Firm
Irvine, California 2001

Brayton + Hughes designed 20,000 square feet on one floor of an existing building in University Research Park to accommodate consultant offices, accelerator space, and shared flex spaces for socializing and food service. Additional program requirements included a reception area, work rooms, and centralized support facilities, as well as satellite conference spaces, copy centers, and storage rooms. The client requested a design that would appeal to their high-tech Southern California clientele while increasing the company's efficiency and flexibility.

The design creates a common entry space that is characterized by high-tech visual media and spatial fragmentation, in keeping with the company's chief clients and the demographics of their workforce. Flanking this space are three interrelated functions: general office space, the accelerator guest offices, and common areas. The common areas are combined with the entry space to create a café/town hall space that brings people together to share ideas and socialize within the office.

Additionally, the design links itself formally with its Southern California location, employing graphic images that echo its seaside setting. Informal circulation is clarified by the open plan, and glass is used on the enclosed private areas, allowing light to circulate throughout the space.

A **The unfinished ceilings and digital supergraphics of the reception lobby give it a high-tech, industrial feel.**

Materials include a mix of concrete floors and carpeting, painted drywall, applied graphic screens, stainless steel, wood and plastic laminate, exposed mechanical systems, and lighting. Furniture systems are Herman Miller Kiva, Etho-Space & Resolve, Knoll Propeller tables and lounge elements, and Brayton sofas.

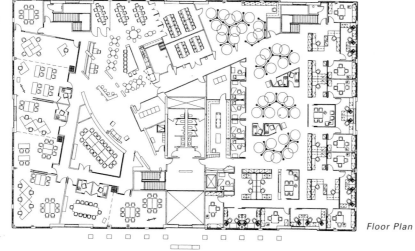

B **The café area has a casual feel, and encourages people from throughout the office to come together.** *C* **Open work areas combine with private team rooms to offer a varying work environment.** *D* **Large graphics used on partitions emphasize the office's Southern California locale.** *E* **Circulation between reception/conference area and offices.**

Floor Plan

Silver Lake Partners
Menlo Park, California 2001

Silver Lake Partners sought a work environment of "quiet confidence," appropriate for a leading private technology-focused equity firm. The founders requested a casual reception area that would assure visitors of Silver Lake's financial prowess. Conference facilities for both meetings and entertaining were a central feature, while private workspaces were needed to underscore the corporate view that all employees are partners in the firm.

The 11,300-square-foot plan separates the public spaces from private spaces, allowing partners the flexibility to either participate in meetings or retreat to their private work sanctuaries. All conference facilities branch off a crescent-shaped reception area. Support services are centralized around the base building core.

Materials for the entry and reception space are beech flooring, Venetian plaster walls, upholstered panels, and stainless steel jambs. The color palette is clean and light, with enough wood and natural materials to maintain a comfortable humanity.

The conference rooms have cove-lighted fabric canopies, centered over custom tables. State-of-the-art technology is provided in the table tops, located below billet aluminum access panels. Sophisticated lighting controls provide proper light for meetings, visual presentations, and dinner events. A video conferencing room provides a 24-hour link to Silver Lake's New York office.

Custom millwork workstations are veneered in eucalyptus and stained ash, with pewter side panels and etched glass transaction tops. The paired office entries are a composition of eucalyptus and carved glass, framed in aluminum and stained ash.

Inside the private offices, the designers created generous custom beech workspaces. Most offices provide lounge seating for informal meetings.

A **The reception area employs beech flooring and a warm, light palette, creating a sense of tranquility and sophistication.**

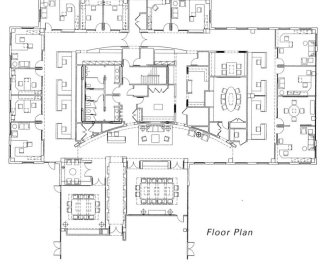

Floor Plan

B Entry hall with reception desk beyond. C This detail of the lobby furnishings suggests a residential quality. D Cove-lighted canopies in the conference rooms give a soft light to the space. E Informal lounges act as break-out rooms for larger conference spaces. F Translucent glass on private offices lets light circulate while retaining a sense of privacy.

F

G *Eucalyptus-veneered custom workstations are combined with etched-glass transaction counters and plate aluminum side panels.*

G

Cooley Godward LLP
Palo Alto, California 2001

Cooley Godward LLP has grown to become one of California's largest law firms by focusing on business and litigation services for the technology sector. As their two-building main office in Palo Alto was becoming crowded, the firm retained Brayton + Hughes to design the interior of another 130,000-square-foot building, providing 70 percent more space. The main program requirements were an efficient and flexible layout, with the maximum number of window offices for attorneys and a corporate café. The project had tight budget restrictions and the interior construction and furnishing process had to be completed within 120 days.

Given the budget and schedule constraints, the architects focused on key areas: the main entry lobby, the typical open office area, and the café. Other spaces were designed to be functional but economical. The main entry lobby features a poured-in-place concrete stair with integrally dyed color and a clear tempered glass guardrail panel. Spanning from the landing across to the second floor is a steel bridge, whose blackened steel guardrail continues around the second floor opening. Flooring is the same green-gold slate used on the building's exterior. Wall surfaces are finished in Venetian plaster and upholstered fabric wall panels.

The designers were challenged to animate the long, narrow space of the typical open office areas. Above the administrative workstations, lowered ceiling planes with pendant fixtures add visual interest, while storage, printers, and files are set back into the interior wall. Recessed entries into attorney's offices are carefully detailed in aluminum and patterned glass. A hand-trowelled Duroplex finish is used on the walls throughout.

The café is the most expressive space in the project. A second story bridge cuts across the double-height room. On one side, the servery and a dining pavilion overlook an outdoor terrace, while on the other side of the bridge the main dining area can be closed off and used as a meeting room. The bridge façades are collages of colored and textured glass.

A secondary project goal was to provide excellent lighting. The open office spaces, conference rooms, and attorney offices incorporate indirect linear fluorescent lighting. Custom fixtures were fabricated for the lobbies and café, and large skylights provide daylight above all six stairs and above the long café bridge.

A The stair in the lobby is composed of dyed poured-in-place concrete and railed with clear tempered glass.

A

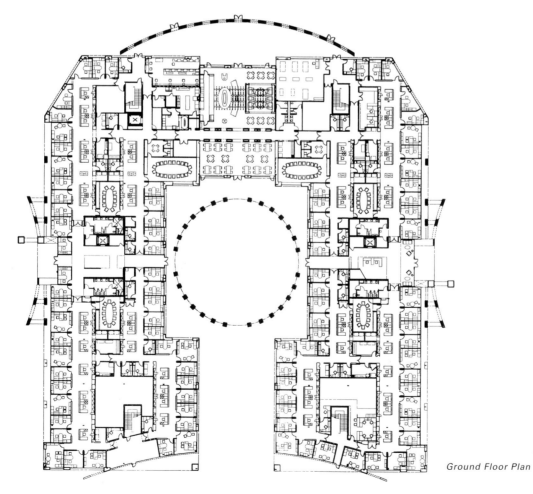

B Strong geometries in the reception desk and the stair maintain a vibrant relationship in the space. C Administrative workstations are organized below custom ceiling panels with indirect lighting. D, E, F, + G The double-height café space is the centerpiece of the project. Areas can be closed off for different functions.

Ground Floor Plan

F G

Schooner's Restaurant
Monterey, California 1998

This program called for a 1,250-square-foot renovation of the lounge at the Monterey Plaza Hotel. The existing lounge was outdated and did not take advantage of the Monterey Bay views. The hotel desired a design that would integrate the exterior and interior designs, and provide a new identity for the bar.

Brayton + Hughes created a unique space with a thematic atmosphere that attracts both tourists and locals to this notable destination along the coast. Challenged by odd geometry, the architects strove to take full advantage of the view and develop a strong connection with the adjacent exterior deck. The result was a bar shape that resembles a sailboat. Abstract details produce a nautical feeling and relate to the name "Schooner's."

The 50-foot bar fits neatly into the existing building shell. A mahogany wall follows the curve of the bar and houses a series of banquette niches that display large murals of hotel luggage stickers from the Italian Riviera. The floor, covered in narrow teak boards with holly wood spacers, mimics the deck of a boat. The bar top, finished in laminated cherry wood, terminates with a large medallion composed of various inlayed woods that form a sailor's compass. Behind the bar, a Douglas fir mast rises from a circular display of bottles and glasses to a boom that stretches toward the bow. A rhythm of colorful back-lit sails gently drape below a midnight blue ceiling that is starlit by fiber optics.

The west side of the bar "boat" appears to be docked at the pier. Different shades of blue concrete tiles are arranged to look like waves. The windows and doors are cased in shutter panels, finished with a patina that connotes a weathered dock house. The west wall has three new pairs of French doors and a large opening that incorporates an exterior bar and can be closed with bi-fold doors. Beyond the shutter wall is the exterior deck, which was newly finished with teak furniture and a shading system.

In addition to the boat details, a sophisticated lighting system, various rich materials, and a colorful furniture scheme all enhance the space. The restaurant's "deck" features small teak tables and yacht chairs. The "dock" uses more substantial rattan chairs and tabletops finished to appear as weathered cedar.

A The yacht-shaped dining room and bar feature teak boat decking and rails, back-lit "sails," and fiber-optic "constellations" set into a midnight blue ceiling. B Above recessed banquettes hang hand-painted posters that resemble old fashioned luggage stickers.

A

C The top of the
bar, which is curved
like the prow of a
boat, is finished in
laminated cherry.
Behind the bar, a
mast-like Douglas
fir pole rises to the
ceiling. D Large
French doors sepa-
rate the outdoor
dining deck and
the bar area.

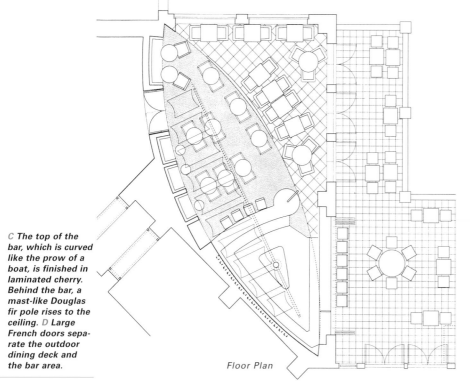

Floor Plan

C

Ritz Carlton Half Moon Bay
Half Moon Bay, California *2001*

Brayton + Hughes was hired to design a luxury hotel on one of the most pristine sites in Northern California. It overlooks the water of Half Moon Bay, which was originally settled by Portuguese fishermen in the 1700s. The resort was conceived as a grand seaside "cottage" in the spirit of Newport, Rhode Island's resorts and residences.

The design strives to be more casual than the typical Ritz Carlton, while maintaining the signature Ritz quality. This sense of gracious hospitality on a residential scale pervades the interior design throughout the hotel. Local traditions and influences are present in the form of Portuguese ceramics and a fine collection of landscape paintings depicting the immediate character of the Northern California coastline.

Materials consist of painted wood, parquet floors, limestone fireplace surrounds, open beam ceilings, classical white moldings, paneled walls, and a tromp l'oeil sky painted into the ceiling dome. The palette and materials reflect the casual seaside cottage theme. The colors are light and airy, and it was important to connect each room to the outdoors. Cotton, chenille, silk, and linen complement the personally scaled rooms, making them casual and comfortable. Simple furnishings, artwork, and accessories create an art collection rather than a specific design theme.

The restaurant's nautical motifs evoke the history of the coastal settlement. The rich mahogany vaulted ceiling, ribbed and lapped in the fashion of a boat hull, is the central feature of the room. The carpet is patterned with a design of abstract rope coils, while brass wall sconces and rope-slung pendants create soft lighting and add to the nautical ambience. Across the room are an open kitchen, a raw bar, and private dining space.

The ballroom pavilion and meeting space, both flexible in size and configuration, continue the theme of a great private estate. Generous prefunction space is furnished with antique consoles, lighting, and art.

Below the main floor is a world class spa designed as a Roman bath and featuring a full aerobics workout facility, individual relaxation living rooms with fireplaces, marble-clad Jacuzzi baths, and steamrooms and saunas. Surrounding these spaces are wet and dry treatment rooms for massage, aromatherapy, and facial and pedicure treatments.

A **The hotel's reception area has an old fashioned, coastal feel.**

A

B The entry rotunda leads to the hotel living room and ocean veranda beyond. C The Ladies' Tea Room is old fashioned and formal. D The barrel-vaulted restaurant is designed with the craftsmanship and materials of fine yachts in mind. E The main library and cigar room also preserve the feel of a hotel of old.

F G

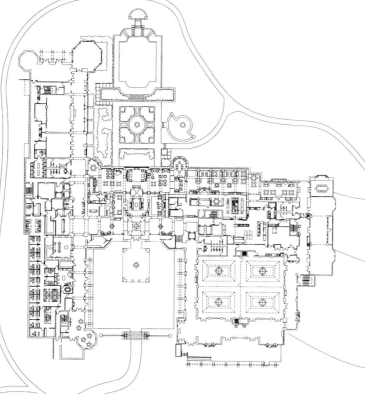

F Bathrooms are intimate, yet luxurious and comfortable. G *The ocean veranda gazes out over the Pacific Ocean.*

Site Plan

Willow Stream Spa
Fairmont Scottsdale Princess Hotel
Scottsdale, Arizona 2002

The program called for a new 35,000-square-foot destination spa at the existing Scottsdale Princess Hotel, that included 18 massage treatment rooms (nine with private massage gardens), three wet treatment rooms, four facial treatment rooms, and one treatment suite. Also included was a rooftop pool, a co-ed waterfall treatment room, separate men's and women's dressing room areas, a cardio-fitness room, an aerobics room, and a salon.

Brayton + Hughes worked together with Three Architecture and Edaw landscape architects to develop the overall concept for the spa, including the architectural organization of the plan and the development of interior ideas. Rather than exploring the architectural themes of the existing hotel, the designers' inspiration for the project was found in the surrounding landscape of the Scottsdale/Phoenix area. Local sandstone walls and floors, mineral water pools, palm trees, and cacti all suggest the soothing and healing powers of the surrounding natural environment.

Working with the spa's director, Brayton + Hughes ensured that the facility would provide the most up-to-date and state-of-the-art spa equipment and facilities, guaranteeing the guest a unique experience with a wide range of treatment opportunities.

A In the entry lobby—with its view to the outdoor courtyard—local sandstone was used on walls and floors, its texture emphasized by hidden lighting.

The interior spaces emphasize the simple richness of natural materials over complex detail and decoration. These finishes included travertine floors, color-washed plaster walls, clear-finished mahogany beams, and rough-cut sandstone walls and fireplaces. Reflecting pools are located throughout the facility to encourage a sense of serenity. The colors and shapes of the surrounding desert inspire fabrics and furnishings.

A

B The guest lounge features a fireplace and similar materials and lighting to the lobby. C The spa's courtyards and gardens allow visitors to enjoy the desert landscape. D Located on the roof, the outdoor pool cascades into the courtyard below, creating a grotto and aqua pressure treatment space. E This typical massage treatment room is at once elegant yet intimate. F The Roman bath in each wet area is a communal cleansing and relaxation space.

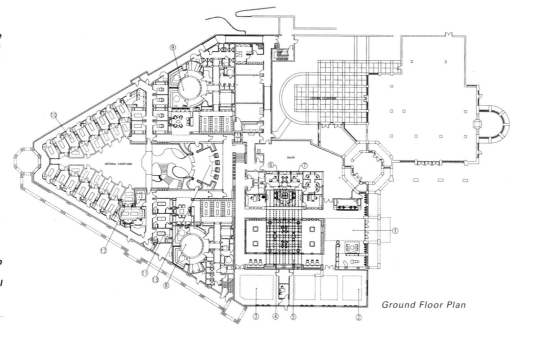

Ground Floor Plan

Four Seasons Resort
Sharm El Sheikh, Egypt 2002

Brayton + Hughes designed this new five-star resort on the Red Sea in Egypt. The program included 140 guestrooms arranged in one- and two-story interconnected buildings, two two-bedroom villas, and one royal presidential villa, in addition to standard hotel suites. The villas are integrated into the steep slopes of Sinai Peninsula to suggest an ancient hillside village. Sited at the top of the hill, the main building houses most public spaces, including the lobby, two restaurants, a ballroom, meeting spaces, a health club, and back-of-house support services. Two additional casual restaurants are located below the resort at seaside, overlooking a private floating marina and the resort's scuba diving facilities.

The resort also includes a residential component, comprising 103 units: 68 two-bedroom "chalets" and 35 four-bedroom private villas. Several other residential units will be used in a hotel rental or time-share program, bringing the total number of units to 276.

The design of the hotel units is sensitive to the surrounding terrain. The architecture utilizes forms and details reminiscent of the hillside towns of North Africa, incorporating powerful domes and Islamic style arches, built of simple brick, plaster, or wood. The lobby is a simple square room with whitewashed plaster walls and a central fountain cut as a granite disc into the floor. The space features a grandly scaled dome, pierced with colored glass openings to the sky.

The restaurants are designed with their own themes, including a Moroccan spice market and a modern Italian dinner club, to give guests a variety of dining experiences. The client requested that several of the restaurants look different than the hotel to create the atmosphere of great metropolitan cities within the resort.

Combining stone floors with color-washed plaster walls, the architects gave the guestrooms and suites a cool, open feeling. Built-in divans are set into niches and colored glass windows at the back of the bedrooms provide interesting light. Each typical room is set up as a suite with a separate bedroom and parlor, a full-sized terrace, and an oversized bath. Fabrics and furnishings are simple, reflecting the sophisticated yet easygoing vernacular of the coastal region.

A The hotel's design takes inspiration from local architecture, with deep loggias and a distinctly North African feel.

A

B The domed reception lobby is an elegant first view into the hotel. C The exterior loggia-lobby lounge allows people to enjoy afternoon tea or drinks. D Here we see the feature of the specialty restaurant, a painting by Omar El Nagdi. E The Royal Suite has a living room for guests to entertain. F The all day restaurant is designed to recall the Arab Souk. G Incorporating Islamic-style domes and arches, the interior's tall ceilings give the spaces a sense of grandeur, such as that of the exterior lobby lounge and bar, pictured here.

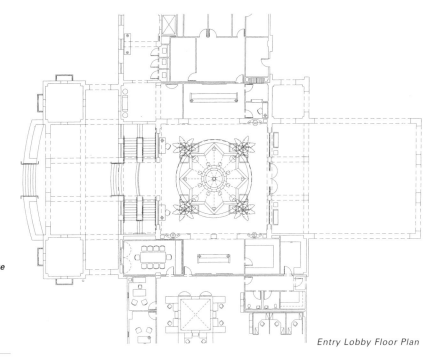

H Typical room bath. I Royal Suite master bedroom. J Typical King Room. K The spa features outdoor hot tubs and private massage rooms.

Entry Lobby Floor Plan

J   K

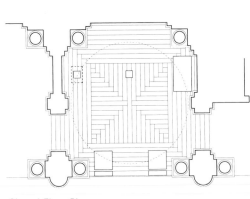

Chapel Floor Plan

The Chapels of St. Ignatius Church
Chapel of Reconciliation
San Francisco, California 1997

Brayton + Hughes designed this chapel of reconciliation for the Jesuit
Catholic parish of St. Ignatius. An enclosed space serves as an alternate
to traditional confession. Here, the confessor has the option of
either speaking to a priest face to face, or speaking in secrecy from
behind a panel.

A wall was constructed to enclose an existing nave, which housed a
small confessional. The confessional was dismantled and reconfigured
to create a movable panel, which would serve to link the old and new
forms of discourse. Stained glass and the architectural forms of the
new wall maintain the existing vocabulary of the cathedral. New and
acquired pieces of artwork and furniture adorn the space.

Materials include plaster, stained glass, and painted drywall. Custom
light fixtures bearing Jesuit-related symbols were designed for the
enclosed space and the adjacent waiting area.

A *View of chapel
from church nave.*
B *Views of domed
ceiling featuring
a stained-glass
oculus symbolizing
the Jesuit faith.*
C *Chapel with
custom-designed
kneelers and a
bronze bust of St.
Ignatius.*

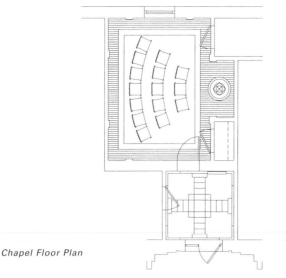

Chapel Floor Plan

The Chapels of St. Ignatius Church
Della Robia Chapel
San Francisco, California 1998

Brayton + Hughes was commissioned by St. Ignatius Church to design a chapel that would commemorate the donors that made the renovation of the church possible. The design concept was to symbolize the transformation of Saint Ignatius.

The transformation is represented within the chapel by freestanding elements in the space. Their placement symbolizes the cycle of his life, and his journeys are represented through movement within the chapel. Rich materials and clean, simple lines maintain a strong symbolism and geometry in the space. In all directions, crosses surround the death mask of Saint Ignatius, signifying his holy relationship with God.

The use of bronze connects the death mask with the surrounding pieces, as its oil-rubbed finish reflects other bronze elements within the church. The warm bronze hue complements the overall palette of the chapel. Horizontal custom-designed pieces of dark-stained Honduras mahogany furniture stand out in silhouette against the bright podium holding the bust. Kneelers rest upon slabs of cast–stained glass, which reflect light from the votive candles and mimic the stained glass oculus (designed by Father Tom Lucas, S.J.) above at the dome's apex. Limestone dominates the central podium, referencing the faux limestone finish on the walls of this and the three adjacent chapels. The volute behind the main podium is a stained birch veneer, directed to emulate the rays that emanate from the inscribed, sandblasted circular medallion. The volute leads upward to the Dutch gold finish dome, which frames the stained glass oculus.

A *View of new Della Robia Chapel from church nave.*
B *This new bronze gate leads to the Baptistry and the Della Robia medallion.*

A

B

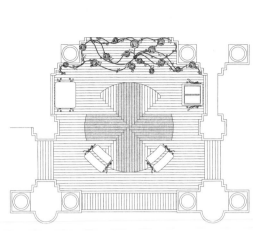

Chapel Floor Plan

The Chapels of St. Ignatius Church
Chapel of Our Lady of Guadalupe
San Francisco, California 2001

Brayton + Hughes renovated an existing nave at St. Ignatius Church into a commemorative chapel dedicated to Our Lady of Guadalupe.

The chapel's main feature is an image of Our Lady of Guadalupe set into an abstract stained birch "tilma." Her image floats above a bronze rose bush sculpture, which holds hand-blown, rose-shaped glass votive candles. In Aztec mythology, the flower symbolizes truth, while these flower votives also reference the flowers that appeared during the apparition. Two kneelers before her visage represent Juan Diego and the bishop Juan Zumarraga.

On one side of the chapel, a bench is provided for the elderly who cannot kneel. A podium, designed with a cast-bonze rose motif, holds a book which tells the translated Aztec version of the story, and provides space for prayers inscribed by those who come to worship. Stars painted on deep blue dome echo the same position of the stars in Mexico City on December 12, 1531, at the moment when Our Lady of Guadalupe appeared to Juan Diego. The stained glass oculus continues the reflection of those stars, with a circle of 12 more stars as a symbolic reference to Mary in Roman Catholic liturgy.

A View of chapel from church nave. B The placement of stars in the plaster dome represent the stars over Mexico City on the morning that Our Lady of Guadalupe appeared. C The painted image of Our Lady of Guadalupe is the main feature of the chapel. The rose-bushes below are cast-bronze.

Stanford University
Main Library Restoration
The Cecil H. Green Library
Bing Wing
Palo Alto, California 2000

The objective of this project was to restore Stanford University's 172,000-square-foot main library, which had been severely damaged in the Loma Prieta earthquake of 1989. Fields Devereaux Architects restored the building structurally, upgraded it mechanically, and integrated current library technology and services. In addition, the renovation improved connections and circulation passages between Green Library West, a neo-Romanesque structure, and Green Library East, very much a mid 20th-century structure.

Brayton + Hughes' design solution reconstructed historically significant elements and spaces. Unsympathetic materials that had been imposed on the building over the years were removed while historic design elements such as columns, plaster ceilings, skylights, doors, and windows were renovated and reinstalled in the building. New elements, including veneer plaster walls and casework, were designed to complement the historic character of the building.

Existing furniture and lighting fixtures were rehabilitated, and new furniture and fixtures were designed to be compatible with the original building's architecture and design. The furniture accommodates "category five" wiring and fiber-optic cable, and brings electrical outlets to virtually every seat in the reconstructed building. Additionally, each of the rooms that could be used for teaching and group study or research was also equipped with coaxial cable so that video sound and images can be played remotely.

New environmental systems were installed, including lighting, HVAC, and state-of-the-art data systems, allowing patrons to plug in for direct access to the internet. These systems were carefully integrated into the historic fabric and structure of the building to help retain and restore its original character. For example, in major public areas the power and data outlets are provided in flush floor outlets, so that furniture can be "unplugged" and moved to different locations. The "plugs" and wires from floor outlets are concealed in the furniture, contained in custom-fabricated power and data outlet boxes integrated into the tabletops. The students never see any of the wires and cables, yet they may conveniently and easily connect to power and the internet at each tabletop and reader seat.

A The monumental stairs extend the main campus axial circulation into the library. B The central rotunda connects to all major reading rooms and stacks, and features new custom light fixtures and a central table.

A

C *Different types of seating are provided in the quiet room, to accommodate students' varying work habits.*

C

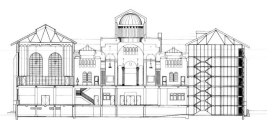

Transverse Section

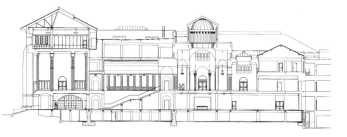

Longitudinal Section

D The entry lobby looks toward the administrative offices. E Here, restoration work on the main reading room is visible, including new lighting and stacks.

Floor Plan

U.S. Federal Courthouse
Fresno, California 2004

The design for the Fresno U.S. Federal Courthouse, a collaboration between Brayton + Hughes, Gruen Associates, and Moore Ruble Yudell Architects, represents a contemporary expression of civic architecture, articulating the program for a federal center of justice. The building consists of 385,000 square feet which accommodate federal courtrooms, jury rooms, justice chambers, U.S. Attorney offices, U.S. Marshall administrative offices, GSA offices, and a variety of conference facilities.

Brayton + Hughes programmed all the project's space and growth requirements, assisted the user groups to define the program's functional requirements, and designed the interior spaces in a vocabulary that consistently expressed the building's architecture. Public circulation spaces were kept purposefully calm, directing interest and drama toward the entry garden and views to the city. Ecologically sound products were evaluated and incorporated into the interior design palette throughout the building.

The design of the courtroom was driven by the desire to create a classically proportioned room accentuated by a sense of verticality. A central barrel vault appears to magically float above the courtroom, adding a sense of formality and focus to the judge's bench while a full-height articulated wood wall serves as its backdrop. Embedded in the wall, a bronze Federal Seal provides a symbolic focal point to the room, and the deep blue carpet gives the courtroom a rich base for the warm maple judicial branch and wainscot. A sculptural wooden ceiling grille, similar to the lobby and gallery ceilings, further distinguishes the judge's bench.

The volumetric organization of the judicial chambers reflects the cadence and fenestration of the building's exterior. Because the chambers are located on the same floor as the courtrooms, ceilings could range in heights from ten to 16 feet. This height was expressed with an asymmetrical cant over each judge's desk, maximizing daylight and views as well as a sense of spaciousness. Various color schemes were developed, individualizing each judge's suite.

A **As demonstrated in this rendering, the building's exterior reflects the interior organization.**

A

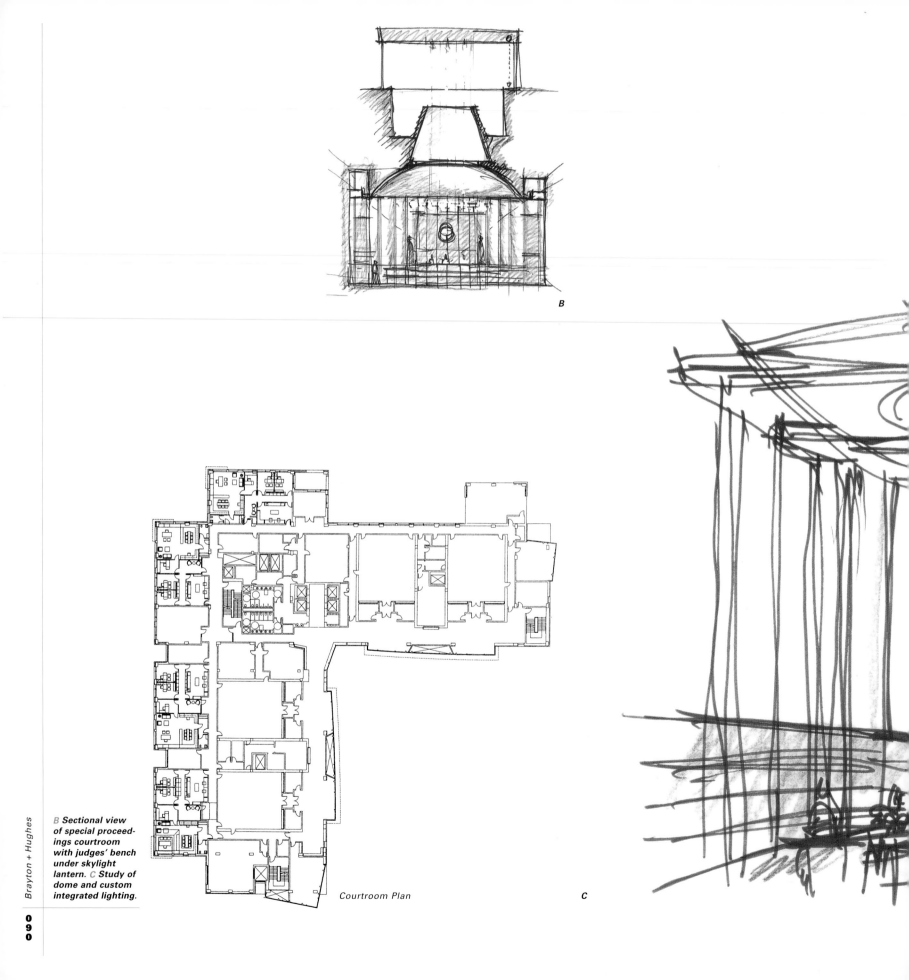

B Sectional view
of special proceed-
ings courtroom
with judges' bench
under skylight
lantern. C Study of
dome and custom
integrated lighting.

B

Courtroom Plan

C

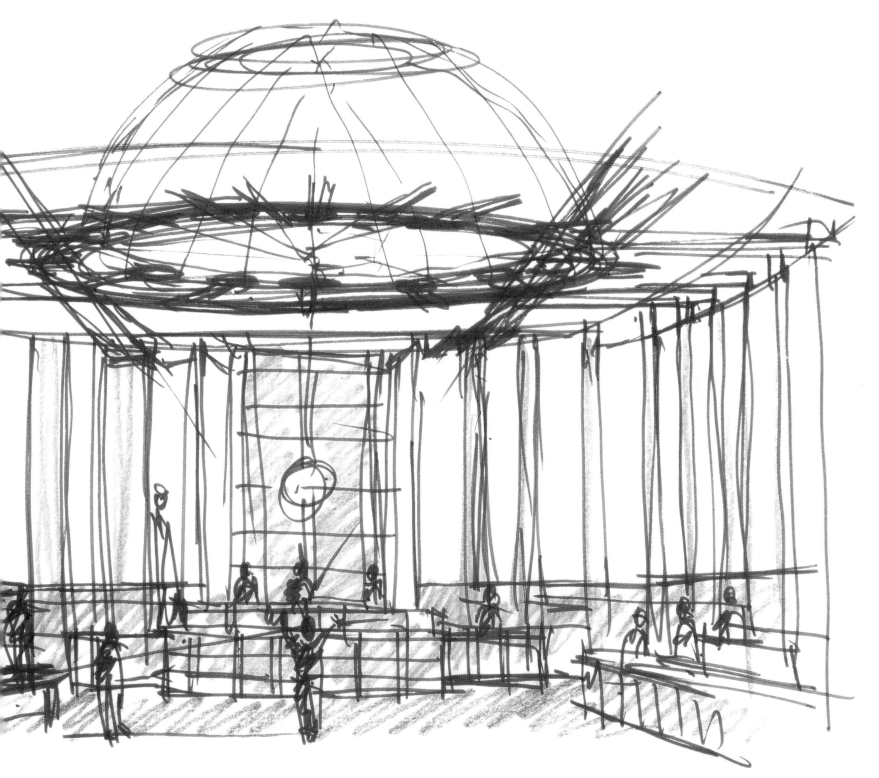

U.S. Embassy
Berlin, Germany 2007

The U.S. Embassy in Berlin occupies a focal position at the center of the reunified Germany. Brayton + Hughes, in concert with Moore Ruble Yudell Architects, designed the new American presence in Berlin to reflect both American values and respect for the people and culture of Germany. Their design was the chosen entry of a national design competition in 1995.

The new embassy stands as both background and partner to the Brandenburg Gate, architecturally reflecting the relationship between the two governments. The copper and glass lantern of the rooftop pavilion serves as a symbolic representation of America's presence. Lit day and night, the pavilion represents the shared democratic values of the United States and Germany, while the scale, details, and materials of the lantern speak to the Quadriga that surmounts the gate.

The Pariser Platz façade opens at its center to reveal the civic-scaled dome of the entry rotunda. A gently curved glass canopy evokes the American flag that flies just above it. The opening of this façade allows the southern sun to stream through, illuminating the flag and extending the space of the platz into the embassy.

From the dignified formality of Pariser Platz to the openness the south porch, the embassy's exterior design responds to conditions at each edge of the site. The formal limestone façade of Pariser Platz is continued but transformed along the Ebertstrasse side. The stricter façade requirements of Pariser Platz are relaxed at the south end, where pergolas, grillwork, and arcades lighten the structure.

Finishes throughout the functional interior spaces foster bright and upbeat environments, but remain modest to meet budgetary goals. A unique feature of the plan is the raised floor plenum, created to replace the traditional ceiling. The walls are thus freed from the usual constraints of ceiling, electrical and mechanical distribution, and structural bearing. As such, they are flexible definers and may be moved easily, without affecting costly building systems. The open ceiling highlights the exposed concrete beams.

The typical department is laid out to maximize daylight and shared views to the exterior. Dark spaces, such as reserve rooms, are inboard, while open office modules are located at the perimeter. Window height is maximized to provide as much natural light as possible. Furniture casework and systems are modular electrified panel design with built-in acoustic performance.

A **North elevation along Eberstrasse, facing the Tiergarten and adjacent to the Brandenburg Gate.**

A

B **The façade at the corner of Eberstrasse and Behrenstrasse features the consulate entry.** C **The"Lodge" is the central gathering space and dining facility, and has access to the open courtyards.** D **The ambassador's State Room has a view to roof garden and Reichstag beyond.**

Boyd Lighting Company— Corporate Offices/Showroom
San Francisco, California 1997

Principal-in-Charge: Richard Brayton, FAIA
Design Team: David Darling, Joel Villalon
Structural Engineer: Kate Simonen, Steve Tipping & Assoc.
General Contractor: Uwe Dobers, Fine European Construction
Client: Jay Sweet, Boyd Lighting Company
Photographer: John Sutton

The Chapels of St. Ignatius Church
San Francisco, California 1997, 1998, & 2001

Principal-in-Charge: Stanford Hughes, FAIA
Design Team: Joel Villalon, Beatriz Martinez,
Jacqueline Lytle, Vincent Chew
General Contractor: Fine Line Group
Client: Father Charles R. Gagan SJ, St. Ignatius Church
Photographer: John Sutton

Chiron Corporation— Life Sciences Building 4
Emeryville, California 1999

Principal-in-Charge: Stanford Hughes, FAIA
Design Team: Joel Villalon, Jacqueline Lytle, David Sun
Associate Architect: Ricardo Legorreta, Legorreta Arquitectos
Structural Engineer: Affiliated Engineers, Inc.
Mechanical Engineer: Affiliated Engineers, Inc.
General Contractor: Rudolph & Sletten, Inc.
Client: Chiron Corporation
Photographer: John Sutton

Cooley Godward LLP
Palo Alto, California 2001

Principal-in-Charge: Richard Brayton, FAIA
Design Team: Jay Adams, AIA, Joel Villalon, Claudine Frasch
Associate Architect: TDM Plan Arquitectos
Structural Engineer: Jack Laws, Structural Design Engineers
Mechanical Engineer: Jeff Fini, Alfa Tech
General Contractor: Devcon Construction, Inc.
Client: Cooley Godward LLP
Photographer: John Sutton

DFS Group Limited— Corporate Headquarters
San Francisco, California 1997

Principal-in-Charge: Stanford Hughes, FAIA
Design Team: Angie Klein, Jacqueline Lytle
Associate Architect: Fee Munson Ebert
General Contractor: C.I.C.
Client: DFS Group Limited, San Francisco
Photographer: John Sutton

Forbes Silicon Valley Bureau
Burlingame, California 2001

Principal-in-Charge: Richard Brayton, FAIA
Design Team: Jay Adams, AIA, Kathleen Johnstone
General Contractor: C.I.C.
Client: Forbes Magazine
Photographer: John Sutton

Four Seasons Resort
Sharm El Sheikh, Egypt 2002

Principal-in-Charge: Richard Brayton, FAIA
Design Team: Melissa Messmer, Nina Chiappa, Lynn Arriola,
Robel Dimaano, Joel Villalon
Associate Architect: Hill Glazier Architects
Client: Talaat Mostafa Group
Photographer: John Sutton

Global Consulting Firm
Irvine, California 2001

Principal-in-Charge: Jay Boothe, AIA
Design Team: Kelly Scott Hill, Michele Koblinsky
General Contractor: Pacific Meridian
Client: Global Consulting Firm
Photographer: Toshi Yoshimi

Global Consulting Firm
Los Angeles, California 2000

Principal-in-Charge: Richard Brayton, FAIA
Design Team: Tim Gemmill, Kelly Scott Hill,
Nina Chiappa, Ross Dugan
General Contractor: Pacific Meridian, Inc.
Client: Global Consulting Firm
Photographer: John Sutton

Global Consulting Firm
Palo Alto, California 2000

Principal-in-Charge: Richard Brayton, FAIA
Design Team: Kelly Scott Hill, Nina Chiappa
Associate Architect: MBT Architecture
Structural Engineer: Sei Structural Engineers, Inc.
Mechanical Engineer: Kinetics
General Contractor: Devcon Construction, Inc.
Client: Global Consulting Firm
Photographer: John Sutton

Pillsbury Madison Sutro—Law Offices
Palo Alto, California 1998

Principal-in-Charge: Richard Brayton, FAIA
Design Team: Rae Hagner, David Darling
Associate Architect: Ken Rodriquez Partners
Structural Engineer: T.K. Lee, LTK Associates
General Contractor: Devcon Construction, Inc.
Client: Pillsbury Madison Sutro, LLP
Photographer: John Sutton

Ritz Carlton Half Moon Bay
Half Moon Bay, California 2001

Principal-in-Charge: Richard Brayton, FAIA, Jay Boothe, AIA
Design Team: Melissa Messmer, Nina Chiappa, Kelly Woods, David Sun
Architect: Hill Glazier Architects
Structural Engineer: Libbey Heywood
General Contractor: L.E.Wentz Company
Client: Vester-Athens/YCP II Half Moon Bay, LLC
Photographer: John Sutton

Schooner's Restaurant
Monterey, California 1998

Principal-in-Charge: Richard Brayton, FAIA
Design Team: Tim Gemmill, David Darling, Kathleen Johnstone
Client: John Narigi, Monterey Plaza Hotel
Photographer: John Sutton

Silver Lake Partners
Menlo Park, California 2001

Principal-in-Charge: Stanford Hughes, FAIA
Design Team: Jay Adams, AIA, Nina Chiappa, Claudine Frasch, Michele Koblinsky, Kathleen Johnstone
Associate Architect: Pablo Mondragon, TDM Arquitectos
Structural Engineer: Jack Laws, Structural Design Engineers
Mechanical Engineers: Leonard Bertolami, ACCO
General Contractor: Devcon Construction, Inc.
Client: Silver Lake Partners
Photographer: John Sutton

Stanford University Main Library Restoration
The Cecil H. Green Library Bing Wing
Stanford University, Palo Alto, California 2000

Principal-in-Charge: Stanford Hughes, FAIA
Design Team: Kris Kawai, Sally Dulude
Associate Architect: Fields Devereaux Architects & Engineers
Structural Engineer: Forell/Elsesser Engineers, Inc.
Mechanical Engineer: Rosenberg & Associates
General Contractor: N.L. Barnes
Client: Stanford University
Photographer: John Sutton

U.S. Embassy
Berlin, Germany 2007

Principal-in-Charge: Richard Brayton, FAIA, Jay Boothe, AIA
Design Team: Stanley Anderson, AIA, Jennifer W. Brannon, AIA, Michele Koblinsky
Associate Architect: Moore Ruble Yudell Architects, Gruen Associates
Mechanical Engineer: Flack + Kurtz, Inc.
Client: U.S. State Department

U.S. Federal Courthouse
Fresno, California 2004

Principal-in-Charge: Stanford Hughes, FAIA
Design Team: Stanley Anderson, AIA, Jacqueline Lytle, Jennifer Todd, Michele Koblinsky, Rae Hagner
Associate Architect: Moore Ruble Yudell Architects, Gruen Associates
Client: General Services Administration

Willow Stream Spa
Fairmont Scottsdale Princess Hotel
Scottsdale, Arizona 2002

Principal-in-Charge: Richard Brayton, FAIA
Design Team: Lorissa Kimm, Laura Cook
General Contractor: Sundt Construction, Inc.
Client: Fairmont Hotels & Resorts
Photographer: John Sutton

Acknowledgments

The Partners of Brayton + Hughes would like to thank our clients for giving us the opportunity to share in the making of some wonderful places.

We would also like to thank our dedicated staff, both past and present, for their devotion to making our projects world class. As of this publication they are:

Jay Adams	Laura Cook	Wenli Lin
Sandy Ahn	Anne-Marie Dalton	Lisa Lorino
Stanley Anderson	Ryan Denny	Beatriz Martinez
Ross Barrow	Robel Dimaano	Drew McKinney
Nicole Benveniste	Michael Embry	Roger Ricketts
Valerie Bergmann	Rachel Fischbach	Amy Rocha
Kathleen Bost	Claudine Frasch	Jennifer Sim
Elisabeth Brandenburg	Jeremy Fried	Glendy Tseng
Jennifer Brannon	Douglas Fu	Joel Villalon
Nina Chiappa	Kris Kawai	Miyuki Yamaguchi
Harry Clay	Michele Kolbinsky	

Finally, we owe a debt of gratitude to our former firms and mentors including, Skidmore, Owings & Merrill, Charles Pfister Associates, and Gruen Associates for their role in our careers as fertile incubators and for their continued support over the years.

Thank You!

Sincerely,
Richard Brayton, FAIA
Stanford Hughes, FAIA
Jay Boothe, AIA
Brayton + Hughes Design Studio, San Francisco

**Left to right:
Richard Brayton,
Jay Boothe, and
Stanford Hughes.**